Man Walks
on the
Moon

D1502625

July 21, 1969

Man Walks
on the
Moon

John Malam

A⁺
Smart Apple Media

First published by Cherrytree Press
(a member of the Evans Publishing Group)
Suite 1,3 Coomb House
7 St Johns Road, Isleworth
Middlesex TW7 6NH, United Kingdom
Copyright © 2003 Evans Brothers Limited
This edition published under license from
Evans Brothers Limited. All rights reserved.

Designed by Neil Sayer, Edited by Julia Bird
Maps by Tim Smith

To contact the author, send an email to:
johnmalam@aol.com

Published in the United States by
Smart Apple Media
1980 Lookout Drive
North Mankato, MN 56003

U.S. publication copyright © 2004 Smart Apple Media
International copyright reserved in all countries.
No part of this book may be reproduced in any form
without written permission from the publisher.
Printed in Hong Kong

Library of Congress Control Number: 2003104659

ISBN 1-58340-407-4

9 8 7 6 5 4 3 2 1

Cover: *Apollo 11* astronaut Buzz Aldrin walks on the
surface of the moon, July 21, 1969.

Note: this book uses times based on Greenwich Mean
Time (GMT), which fixes the time and date of Armstrong's
first step on the moon at 2:56 A.M., on July 21, 1969.
In American Eastern Standard Time, the event occurred
at 9:56 P.M., on July 20, 1969.

Picture credits:
Corbis: front cover, 11, 15, 16, 18, 19, 20, 23, 24, 25, 27,
28, 30, 31, 32, 33, 34, 35, 36, 37, 38, 39
David King Collection: 21
Science Photo Library: 26
Topham Picturepoint: 12, 13, 17, 22, 29

Contents

The Race to Space

Humankind has always dreamed of traveling in space. The idea of being able to fly to the moon, let alone walk on its surface, seemed to be little more than **science fiction** until the **space race** began in the late 1950s.

The space race grew out of the ongoing power struggle between the two world superpowers of the time, the United States of America and the **Soviet Union**. This power struggle was known as the **Cold War**, because unlike a physical war involving actual fighting, the Cold War was limited to political tension. Beginning in 1945, following the end of the Second World War, it stemmed from the very different politics of the two superpowers. It created an atmosphere of mutual suspicion and rivalry, which led to each side trying to outdo each other, particularly in terms of military strength.

Russian and American leaders photographed in 1959, when Russia led the space race.

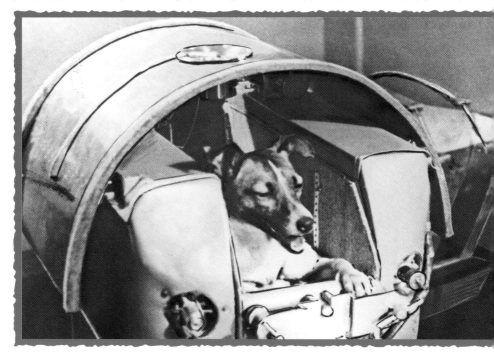

Laika, the Russian dog sent into space in November 1957.

The space race was just another way in which the Cold War was played out, with each side wanting to show it had the technology and skill to beat the other. At first, there was no real goal or end to the space race, and each side's successes were marked by the number of times they achieved something before their rivals.

The Soviet Union dominated the early years of the space race, taking the lead in October 1957 when it launched *Sputnik 1*. This was the world's first artificial **satellite**—a tiny aluminum sphere that flew around the Earth. *Sputnik 2* followed in November of the same year, taking the first living creature into space, a dog named Laika.

In 1959, the Soviet *Luna 3* space probe took the first photographs of the far side of the moon. These events were broadcast worldwide, to the amazement of all.

In April 1961, the Soviet Union made history when Yuri Gagarin became the first person in space. Several weeks before, a dummy had **orbited** the Earth in a spacecraft to test the rocket and the spacesuit that Gagarin would wear on his mission. Before his flight, Gagarin said he was "glad, proud, happy—as any Soviet man would be." He circled the Earth once on board *Vostok 1*, in a flight that lasted just 108 minutes, and instantly became a Soviet hero.

Russian cosmonauts Valentina Tereshkova (the first woman in space) and Yuri Gagarin (the first man in space).

Kennedy's Pledge

There was great pressure on the United States not to fall behind its Soviet rivals in the space race. The US had launched its first successful satellite, *Explorer 1*, in 1958, the same year that the National Aeronautics and Space Administration (NASA) was founded. But Gagarin's space flight came as a major blow to the Americans. They wanted to prove to the world that the US was as strong a power as the Soviet Union, and was still in the space race.

On May 5, 1961, less than four weeks after Gagarin's historic flight, Alan Shepard became the first US **astronaut**. His flight, which took him 116 miles (186 km) above the Earth's surface, lasted just 15 minutes.

The headquarters of NASA—the center for space exploration.

John F. Kennedy, president of the US from 1960 to 1963. He pledged that America would land a man on the moon.

After much debate between politicians, it was decided that the United States could be the first nation to put a man on the moon, beating the Soviet Union to it. On May 25, 1961, just 20 days after Shepard's flight, the president of the US, John F. Kennedy, made a famous speech, in which he said:

"I believe that this nation should commit itself to achieving the goal, before this decade is out, of landing a man on the moon and returning him safely to Earth. No single space project . . . will be more exciting . . . or more important . . . and none will be so difficult or expensive to accomplish."

In other words, President Kennedy was making an extraordinary claim—that the US would put a man on the moon within nine years.

Early Space Missions

Initially, the main aim for both the Soviet Union and the United States was to find out if human beings could survive in space. No one knew how the human body would cope with the impact of takeoff and landing, or the effects of weightlessness. It was also not known whether astronauts would suffer any ill effects after returning to Earth.

The seven American astronauts who took part in the Mercury space program (see page 17).

Between 1961 and 1963, the United States tested the effects of space flight on the human body in a series of six manned flights. Astronauts flew into space inside a tiny Mercury spacecraft, the American answer to the Soviet Union's Vostok craft. Mercury was a cone-shaped space vehicle, just 9.5 feet (2.9 m) long, with room inside for one astronaut. Unlike today's computer-controlled spacecraft, the Mercury astronauts controlled their vehicles manually, by pressing buttons, flicking switches, and pulling levers.

One of the first aims of the Mercury space program was to orbit a manned spacecraft around Earth, as Gagarin had done four years previously. This was accomplished on February 20, 1962, when Lieutenant Colonel John Glenn became the first American astronaut to circle the Earth in *Mercury 6*.

The Mercury flights ended in May 1963, when Major L. Gordon Cooper made 22 Earth orbits in *Mercury 9*. He had spent more than 34 hours in space—a record for an American astronaut, and important proof that the human body could survive for a long period of time in space.

Major L. Gordon Cooper, on his return to Earth after his flight in **Mercury 9.**

The Gemini Missions

When the US Mercury space program ended, a bolder one began. This was the Gemini space program, introduced in 1964. The Gemini spacecraft was larger than the one used in the Mercury missions, and could take two astronauts at a time into space. Between 1965 and 1966, 10 Gemini space flights took place, testing the procedures needed to ensure a safe passage to the moon. Astronauts practiced **docking** with other spacecraft and walking in space. The Gemini astronauts also spent much longer in space than the Mercury astronauts had. This was because NASA needed to be sure a space crew could stand the effects of being in space for up to two weeks—the time it would take to fly to the moon and back.

On June 3, 1965, Ed White became the first US astronaut to walk in space, during the **Gemini 6** *space flight.*

The wreckage of a training vehicle, from which Neil Armstrong parachuted to safety in 1968.

The Gemini space program gathered a large amount of essential information that would help NASA in the race to be the first superpower to send an astronaut safely to the moon. However, not all missions went according to plan. On March 16, 1966, *Gemini 8* was launched. The pilot was Neil A. Armstrong, and his copilot was Captain David R. Scott. The mission was scheduled to last three days, and would include the first US docking in space with an unmanned spacecraft. But a fault with the **thrusters** meant that, after docking, *Gemini 8* went spinning out of control. Only Armstrong's quick reactions and clear thinking prevented a disaster. *Gemini 8* returned to Earth less than 11 hours after takeoff.

Moon Rockets

In contrast to the Americans, the leaders of the Soviet Union had never publicly declared their intention to land a man on the moon. With the mistrust typical of the Cold War era, the Soviets were much more secretive about their space program, and its achievements and setbacks were rarely publicized. Despite this, it did become known that they were building a rocket powerful enough to blast a spacecraft to the moon, and bring it back to Earth.

Nikita Khrushchev, leader of the Soviet Union, and figurehead of its space program from 1953–1964.

The moon rocket designed by the Soviet Union was the *N-1*. It was first launched in February 1969, but a fire in one of its engines caused the rocket to crash just a minute after liftoff. A second *N-1* was launched in July 1969. It turned out to be a huge disaster for the Soviet space program.

The giant rocket, loaded with fuel, fell back onto its launch pad just seconds after liftoff. It exploded instantly, causing a massive amount of damage to the launch site. Fortunately both *N-1* missions were unmanned, but the effects of the crashes were nevertheless devastating, effectively dashing any hopes the Soviets may still have had of being the first power to land a man on the moon.

At the same time, the Americans were finalizing the design of the *Saturn 5* moon rocket. It was to be the biggest, most powerful rocket ever launched.

A postcard commemorating the Soviet space program.

The Apollo Space Program

Apollo 9 *on the launch pad in 1969.*

NASA used the mighty *Saturn 5* rocket to launch a new spacecraft, called Apollo. It was bigger than any craft previously built by the United States, and was designed to hold three astronauts. The Apollo space program began in 1967, using the wealth of information gathered by the Mercury and Gemini missions. The ultimate aim of Apollo was to land men on the moon, and return them safely home to Earth.

The Apollo spacecraft consisted of three sections or modules—a **command module**, a **service module**, and a **lunar module**. Each module had a specific task to do. The command module was where the crew lived and worked, the lunar module was the section that would land on the moon, and the service module supplied the Apollo with essential oxygen, water, and fuel.

The plan was that, once in orbit around the moon, the lunar module would separate from the other two modules. One astronaut would stay in orbit in the command module, while the other two astronauts landed on the moon in the lunar module. Later, the two astronauts would lift off from the moon's surface in the lunar module and dock with the command module. All three men would then fly back to Earth.

But even the most carefully made plans can go wrong. The Apollo space program was soon to discover this, to its cost.

Parts of an Apollo spacecraft on display at the Kennedy Space Center, Florida.

Disaster . . . and Success

In January 1967, at the very start of the Apollo space program, disaster struck. The three astronauts who were scheduled to fly in *Apollo 1*, the first mission of the new program, were killed during training. They were inside the Apollo for a routine training exercise when a fire broke out. The air inside the spacecraft was made of pure oxygen—the perfect fuel for a fire. One man had time to shout "Fire!" Nothing else was heard, and all three men were dead within seconds. This was the first American spacecraft accident to end in loss of life. As a result, the Apollo space program was almost abandoned,

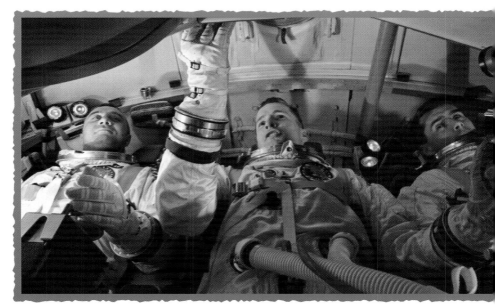

Roger Chaffee, Ed White, and Virgil Grissom, who died in the Apollo 1 accident.

and NASA extensively redesigned the interior of the spacecraft to prevent such an accident from ever happening again.

The tragedy meant many months' delay for future Apollo missions, but on December 21, 1968, *Apollo 8* lifted off from the Kennedy Space Center, Florida. Its mission was to fly to the moon, a distance of 233,014 miles (375,000 km). This was not a mission to land men on the moon. Instead, its crew planned to orbit it, looking for a good site for future astronauts to land.

On Christmas Eve 1968, *Apollo 8* approached to within 70 miles (112 km) of the moon's surface. The astronauts flew around the Moon 10 times, taking photographs of its surface, before setting off on the long flight back to Earth.

Apollo 8 *lifts off on its mission to orbit the moon.*

The Soviet Union Out of the Space Race

Although the *N-1* disaster had forced the Soviet Union to suspend its plans for sending a man to the moon, its space program continued. With their Luna program, the Soviets concentrated on sending unmanned spacecraft to the moon to collect data about its environment, which could be used in the planning of future manned missions. In February 1966, the Soviets had an important success when the *Luna 9* mission made the first unmanned landing ever on the moon.

In September 1968, the Soviet Union launched a spacecraft called *Zond 5*. On board were a variety of life forms—turtles, bacteria, plants, and seeds. These became the first living things from Earth to reach the moon and fly around it, before returning safely to our planet.

The far side of the Moon, photographed by cosmonauts on the **Luna 3** *mission.*

The Soviet Union wanted to show the world it could still compete with the US in the space race, and on July 13, 1969 it sent a new spacecraft hurtling toward the moon. *Luna 15* was another unmanned vehicle that was designed to land on the moon, collect soil and rock samples, and bring them back to Earth. Unfortunately, *Luna 15* crash-landed on the moon's surface—another costly blow to the Soviet space program.

There was now only one country left in the space race, and just three days after *Luna 15* was launched, a new mission from the US blasted into space. It was *Apollo 11*.

Newspapers in the Soviet Union reported the news of the failed Luna 15 *mission.*

Apollo 11

Apollo 11 lifted off from the Kennedy Space Center on July 16, 1969, watched by an audience of millions. This was the mission the whole world had been waiting for—the mission that would put a man on the moon before the end of the 1960s, just as President Kennedy had promised.

On board Apollo 11 was a crew of three: Commander Neil A. Armstrong, Edwin "Buzz" Aldrin, and Michael Collins. All three men were skilled and experienced astronauts. They had all worked as **test** or fighter **pilots** for the US Air Force before joining NASA, and had all taken part in the original Gemini space program. Indeed, it was Neil Armstrong's quick reactions that had averted disaster when the Gemini 8 spacecraft lost control during a test mission.

Apollo 11's historic mission begins.

The crew of **Apollo 11** *(from left): Neil Armstrong, Michael Collins, and Buzz Aldrin.*

Nothing, however, could have fully prepared the astronauts for the importance of the mission that they were about to undertake.

The enormous *Saturn 5* rocket first took the astronauts into orbit around the Earth. Then a blast or "burn" from its own engines propelled *Apollo 11* free of Earth's **gravity**, and it headed for the moon.

It took three days for the tiny spacecraft to reach the moon, and once it did, it went into orbit around it. *Apollo 11* circled the moon 14 times in total, giving its crew time to prepare for their historic landing.

The Moon Landing

The time soon came for the lunar module, named *Eagle*, to separate from the command module, *Columbia*. With the help of another engine burn, the *Eagle* headed for the moon's surface. Inside were Neil Armstrong and Buzz Aldrin. Michael Collins stayed in *Columbia*, which continued to orbit the moon.

Buzz Aldrin preparing for the moon landing.

The *Eagle* flew to a region of the moon's surface known as the Sea of Tranquillity. A landing area, which was about the size of a football field and littered with rocks, had already been chosen, and the *Eagle* headed straight for it. It was a difficult descent, and as the *Eagle* neared the surface, Armstrong took over from the craft's **automatic pilot**, which was about to land it at a very rocky site. Armstrong maneuvered the *Eagle* to a smoother landing place, some 4 miles (6 km) from the original site. When the *Eagle* touched down, it had just 45 seconds' worth of fuel left.

The date was July 20, 1969, and the time was 8:17 P.M. **Greenwich Mean Time (GMT)**. The first words reported back to Earth from the surface of the moon were those of Commander Neil Armstrong, who said: "Houston. Tranquillity Base here. The *Eagle* has landed."

From the moment of liftoff, it had taken 102 hours and 45 minutes for Armstrong and Aldrin to land on the moon. It was almost time for them to step out onto its surface and make history.

The **Apollo 11** *lunar module makes its descent to the moon's surface.*

July 21, 1969

The *Eagle* had to be ready for takeoff again as soon as possible in case of an emergency, and for the next two hours, the astronauts prepared the module for its return flight to *Columbia*. After a meal, they were supposed to rest, but they were too excited and asked instead if they could go out onto the moon's surface earlier than planned. The flight control center at Houston, Texas, agreed, and Armstrong and Aldrin spent the next few hours preparing for man's first steps on the moon.

At 2:59 A.M. GMT, 39-year-old Neil Armstrong descended the ladder of the *Eagle*. A television camera positioned on the outside of the craft recorded the historic moment when he became the first human being to step onto the surface of the moon.

Neil Armstrong steps onto the moon's surface—the first man on the moon.

Millions of people all over the world watched their television sets as fuzzy black-and-white pictures were sent back to Earth. They were watching history in the making. As Armstrong took his first step on the moon's dusty gray surface, he said these famous words: "That's one small step for man, one giant leap for mankind."

He was soon joined by Aldrin, and the two astronauts spent two and a half hours walking on the moon. They collected rock and soil samples, took photographs, and set up equipment to collect scientific data. Finally, they erected a US flag to commemorate America's famous victory in the space race and man's first visit to the moon.

Buzz Aldrin stands by the American flag at Tranquillity Base.

Apollo 11's Return and Beyond

After almost a day on the moon, the *Eagle* lifted off from the moon and flew up to dock with *Columbia*. The three astronauts were reunited, and the journey home to Earth began. All went smoothly, and three days later, on July 24, 1969, *Apollo 11* splashed down in the Pacific Ocean. The astronauts were taken on board the aircraft carrier *Hornet*, and put straight into **quarantine**

Splashdown for **Apollo 11's** *command module.*

The **Apollo 11** *crew in quarantine, following their historic flight to the moon.*

for three weeks to make sure they had not returned with unknown microorganisms that might be dangerous to life on Earth.

Apollo 11 had successfully completed its historic mission. It had taken men to the moon and brought them safely home, along with soil and rock samples and groundbreaking photographs. Armstrong, Aldrin, and Collins had been away from Earth for just nine days—nine days that had changed their lives and the course of history. They were hailed as heroes, not only in the United States, but all over the world. US President Richard Nixon claimed the occasion as "the greatest in the history of the world since Creation."

Other Apollo Missions

In the years following *Apollo 11*'s historic lunar landing, there were another six manned moon missions, five of which succeeded in landing men on the moon. Only *Apollo 13* failed in its mission. An explosion in an oxygen tank in the service module meant that its moon landing had to be canceled—and almost led to a much greater disaster. It was only through the skill of the astronauts and Houston ground staff that the astronauts were able

*The story of **Apollo 13** was made into a blockbuster movie starring actor Tom Hanks, pictured here.*

to return to Earth safely. *Apollo 17* was the last mission to send men to the moon. Its astronauts walked on the moon's surface in December 1972. Since then, no one has yet been back.

A total of 12 US astronauts walked on the moon during the Apollo space program. The missions that completed moon landings collected a huge amount of important information about the planet, and almost 880 pounds (400 kg) of soil and rock samples were collected.

Harrison Schmitt, the last man on the moon, photographed in 1972.

An End to the Race

Since the last of the Apollo missions in 1972, space exploration has moved in other directions. The Apollo missions were expensive, and many people began to question what their overall purpose was. The US space program was reduced in size, and the search began to find cheaper methods of space flight. The result was the Space Shuttle, a space vehicle that can be reused many times. It was first launched in 1981.

*Russian space station **Mir**, seen in orbit above the Earth in 1995.*

Other advances have also been made. We now have the technology to live in space for long periods, as shown by the cosmonauts and astronauts who lived in the Russian *Mir* space station for months at a time. We even have space tourists—in 2001 American millionaire Dennis Tito became the first civilian to pay for a trip into space when he visited the International Space Station. But none

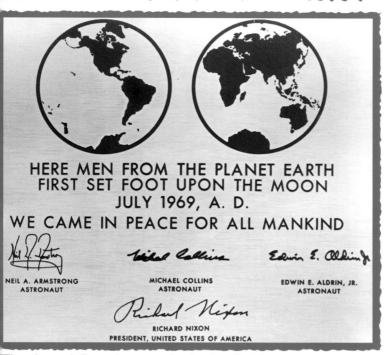

HERE MEN FROM THE PLANET EARTH
FIRST SET FOOT UPON THE MOON
JULY 1969, A. D.
WE CAME IN PEACE FOR ALL MANKIND

NEIL A. ARMSTRONG
ASTRONAUT

MICHAEL COLLINS
ASTRONAUT

EDWIN E. ALDRIN, JR.
ASTRONAUT

RICHARD NIXON
PRESIDENT, UNITED STATES OF AMERICA

The plaque left on the moon by the **Apollo 11** *astronauts.*

of this compares with the excitement of the space
race and the moment that Neil Armstrong first stepped
onto the moon.

When *Apollo 11* lifted off from the moon in July 1969,
the astronauts left a small plaque behind. On it are
written these words:

Here men from the planet Earth
first set foot upon the moon
July 1969, A.D.
We came in peace for all mankind

Timeline

1957	*October 4: Sputnik 1*, the first artificial satellite, is launched.
1957	*November 3:* Laika, a Soviet dog, is the first living creature in space.
1958	NASA (National Aeronautics and Space Administration) is set up in US.
1961	*April 12:* Yuri Gagarin, a Soviet cosmonaut, is the first person in space.
1961	*May 25:* President Kennedy vows US will put a man on the moon by the end of the decade.
1963	*June 16–19:* The Soviet Union's Valentina Tereshkova is the first woman in space.
1965	*March 18:* Alexei Leonov, a Soviet cosmonaut, completes the first space walk.
1966	*February 3:* Unmanned Soviet spacecraft *Luna 9* makes the first soft moon landing.
1966	*March 31:* Unmanned Soviet spacecraft *Luna 10* completes the first orbit of the moon.
1966–67	US Lunar Orbiters map the moon's surface.
1967	*April:* Unmanned US *Surveyor 3* collects moon dust.
1968	*December 24:* The US *Apollo 8* makes the first manned orbit of the moon.
1969	*July 21: Apollo 11* US astronaut Neil Armstrong is the first person to walk on the moon.

1969	November 19: Apollo 12 completes second manned moon landing.
1970	April: Apollo 13 lunar landing canceled due to technical failure.
1971	February 5: Apollo 14 makes third manned landing.
1971	July 30: Apollo15 performs fourth manned landing. Astronauts drive a Lunar Roving Vehicle across the surface of the moon.
1972	April 21: Apollo 16 performs fifth manned landing.
1972	December 19: Apollo 17, the sixth and last manned mission to land on the moon, splashes back down to Earth.

Men who have walked on the moon

Astronaut	Mission	Date
1. Neil Armstrong	Apollo 11	1969
2. Edwin "Buzz" Aldrin	Apollo 11	1969
3. Charles Pete Conrad	Apollo 12	1969
4. Alan Bean	Apollo 12	1969
5. Alan Shepard	Apollo 14	1971
6. Edgar Mitchell	Apollo 14	1971
7. David Scott	Apollo 15	1971
8. James Irwin	Apollo 15	1971
9. John Young	Apollo 16	1972
10. Charles Duke	Apollo 16	1972
11. Gene Cernan	Apollo 17	1972
12. Harrison Schmitt	Apollo 17	1972

Glossary

astronaut A person who travels in space. (From the Greek words *astron,* meaning "star" and *nautes,* meaning "sailor.")

automatic pilot A device in an aircraft or spacecraft that automatically flies the vehicle, without a person at the controls.

Cold War The time from the end of the Second World War (1945) to the breakup of the Soviet Union (1991), when tension between the US and the Soviet Union could have led to war.

command module The part of an Apollo spacecraft in orbit around the moon.

cosmonaut A Russian astronaut. (From "cosmos" and "astronaut.")

docking When two or more space vehicles join together in space.

gravity The powerful force in the universe that pulls objects toward each other.

Greenwich Mean Time (GMT) The time at Greenwich, London. It is used as a basis for calculating time throughout the world.

lunar Having to do with the moon. (From the Latin word *luna,* meaning "moon.")

lunar module The part of an Apollo spacecraft that landed on the moon.

orbit To fly all the way around a body in space, such as a spacecraft or satellite traveling around the moon or the Earth.

quarantine When a person or animal is deliberately isolated from others, to prevent disease from spreading.

satellite Any object that orbits a planet. The moon is a satellite of planet Earth. A communications satellite is a man-made satellite that is sent into orbit around the Earth.

science fiction A made-up story that uses science in the plot. Science fiction stories are often set in space.

service module The part of an Apollo spacecraft that supplied the vehicle with oxygen, water, and fuel.

Soviet Union A group (union) of East European nations, the most powerful of which was Russia. It broke up in 1991, and the nations emerged as separate self-governing countries.

space race The name given to the race between the US and the Soviet Union to be the first to achieve set goals in space. The ultimate goal was to be first to land a man on the moon.

test pilot A person who flies new types of aircraft, testing them to find out how well they work.

thruster A rocket on a spacecraft that gives it the power to move in space.

Index